T0387496

EXTREME COLD AND
BLIZZARDS

by Marcia Abramson

BEARPORT
PUBLISHING

Minneapolis, Minnesota

Bearport Publishing Company Product Development Team

President: Jen Jenson; Director of Product Development: Spencer Brinker; Managing Editor: Allison Juda; Associate Editor: Naomi Reich; Associate Editor: Tiana Tran; Senior Designer: Colin O'Dea; Associate Designer: Elena Klinkner; Associate Designer: Kayla Eggert; Product Development Specialist: Anita Stasson

Produced for Bearport Publishing by BlueAppleWorks Inc.
Managing Editor for BlueAppleWorks: Melissa McClellan
Art Director: T.J. Choleva
Photo Research: Jane Reid

Library of Congress Cataloging-in-Publication Data is available at www.loc.gov or upon request from the publisher.

ISBN: 979-8-88509-982-0 (hardcover)
ISBN: 979-8-88822-162-4 (paperback)
ISBN: 979-8-88822-302-4 (ebook)

For more information, write to Bearport Publishing, 5357 Penn Avenue South, Minneapolis, MN 55419.
Printed in the United States of America.

Contents

Snowbound

It starts with just a few small flakes floating through the air. But soon, the wind begins to gust and howl. Within hours it's snowing so hard that you can barely see a few feet outside your window. The wind is even whipping the falling flakes sideways. It's a blizzard! You try to open the front door, but the snowdrifts are so high that it won't budge. That's some seriously extreme winter weather.

A blizzard is a severe snowstorm with high winds and low **visibility**.

WHAT A DAY TO PICK FOR A WALK!

NO KIDDING!

Blizzard winds can reach more than 120 miles per hour (193 kph). That's as strong as a medium-sized hurricane.

When you can see almost nothing in front of you because of blowing snow, **you are in a whiteout**.

WHAT A WHITEOUT! LET'S GET TO A SHELTER!

IT MIGHT JUST BE A SHORT SQUALL.

Snow **squalls** are brief mini-blizzards. Squalls cause whiteouts but blow themselves out in less than an hour.

Sometimes, ground blizzards pick up after snow stops falling. Strong winds blow snow that has already collected on the ground.

Blizzards can sometimes be joined by thundersnow—when heavy snowfall is coupled with thunder and lightning.

IS THAT THUNDERSNOW HEADED OUR WAY?

I HOPE NOT! A REGULAR BLIZZARD IS BAD ENOUGH!

Chill Out!

Even before the blinding snow, the first thing you will probably notice about a blizzard is the cold. Blizzards can't form without below-freezing temperatures. The air must be cold enough to freeze water droplets into snowflakes. Add winds to this winter weather and everything starts to feel that much colder. That's thanks to windchill!

Cold air can feel even colder on your skin **because of windchill.**

Meteorologists measure windchill by combining temperature and wind speed. **Windchill kicks in when winds are faster than 3 miles per hour (5 kph).**

I WISH THIS WINDCHILL WOULD CHILL OUT ALREADY!

Windchill affects animals as well as people.

The coldest windchills in U.S. history were recorded in New Hampshire in 2023. It felt like -108 degrees Fahrenheit (-78 degrees Celsius).

The coldest air temperature recorded in Antarctica was -144°F (-98°C). That's not even counting windchill!

Wobbly Winds

The cold air and strong winds that are needed to create blizzards are sometimes brought in by weather from the north. A band of winds, called a **vortex**, is always swirling above the North Pole in a counterclockwise direction. The **rotation** of the winds helps keep cold polar air bottled up within the Arctic Circle. But sometimes the tight spinning of the vortex wobbles and breaks down. Then, the **frigid** air of the polar vortex pours south into North America.

The polar vortex is at its strongest during the winter. Its winds blow at more than 100 miles per hour (160 kph).

WHERE'RE YOU GOING?

Meteorologists believe the polar vortex has been swirling frigid winds around the Arctic for more than four billion years.

SOUTH! SOMEWHERE WARMER.

YEAH, WE'VE HAD IT WITH THIS COLD POLAR VORTEX!

Polar dinosaurs, such as the turkey-sized hypsilophodont and a flying reptile called a pterosaur, lived in frigid places that had snowy and icy weather.

On February 14, 2021, a polar vortex sent freezing air into Texas, causing millions of people to lose power.

SOME VALENTINE'S DAY! LET'S GO SOMEWHERE WARM.

WE ARE! I BOUGHT US TWO PLANE TICKETS TO ALASKA!

During the same week of the Valentine's Day freeze, it was warmer in parts of Alaska, Greenland, Norway, and Sweden than it was in Texas.

Alberta Clippers, Saskatchewan Screamers, and Manitoba Maulers are weather patterns that bring snow from the Canadian Rockies to the Atlantic Ocean.

The South Pole has a polar vortex, too. It's stronger than the Arctic one and doesn't wobble as much.

WHERE DID THIS LOUD SNOWSTORM COME FROM?

IT CAME SCREAMING ALL THE WAY FROM SASKATCHEWAN.

Heat in Retreat

If a polar vortex brings freezing winds to your town, you'd better bundle up against the extreme cold! Stay out in freezing weather too long, and your body temperature will begin to drop. When you lose heat faster than your body can make it, an illness called hypothermia sets in. It stops your heart, brain, and other organs from working well. Eventually, it can lead to death. *Yikes!* How can we fight this dangerous condition?

Shivering is your body's way to stay warm. The twitching of your muscles helps create heat and raises your body temperature.

I TOLD YOU TO WEAR A HAT! YOU'RE SHIVERING ALL OVER.

LET'S GET HIM INSIDE BEFORE HE GETS HYPOTHERMIA!

Your normal body temperature is 98.6°F (37°C). Hypothermia sets in when your temperature slips below 95°F (35°C).

While waiting for medical help for hypothermia, have the person remove any wet clothing, wrap up in dry blankets, and sip warm drinks.

To treat hypothermia, doctors take blood out of your body, warm it in special machines, and then put it back into you.

When your skin and the tissues beneath it freeze, they can become damaged. This is called frostbite.

Sun can still pack a punch during the winter. It reflects off the snow and may cause a sunburn even when it's cold outside.

Snowstorm Supersized

When it's cold enough to get frostbite and the snow is coming down hard, you may think you're facing a blizzard. But a blizzard is all about wind speed. To be called a blizzard in the United States, a snowstorm must have winds over 35 miles per hour (55 kph) that blow steadily for at least 3 hours. These winds carry snow, creating a swirling curtain of white that makes it impossible to see more than a quarter of a mile (400 m) ahead of you. Now that's a real blizzard!

The word *blizzard* used to mean a round of cannonfire or gunfire. Americans first began using it for snow in the 1800s.

WHAT A HORRIBLE SNOWSTORM. I CAN'T SEE A THING.

IT'S NOT JUST ANY SNOWSTORM. IT'S A BLIZZARD!

Blizzards can create snowdrifts that are over 50 feet (15 m) high. That's as tall as a five-story building!

The huge Groundhog Day storm of 2011 created blizzard conditions that stretched all the way from New Mexico into Eastern Canada.

More than 21 inches (53 cm) of snow fell on Chicago during the Groundhog Day blizzard. It was the city's third-largest snowfall on record.

Bomb cyclones bring winter weather to the Great Lakes and the East Coast of the United States.

YOU NEED TO IMPROVISE, PEOPLE!

In December 2022, a bomb cyclone brought winds raging at 80 miles per hour (130 kph) to New York City, along with blowing snow and freezing rain.

Blizzard Country

Blizzards are all about wind and **air pressure**. They form when warm, high pressure and cold, low pressure meet. In central parts of the United States and Canada, colder air from the Arctic and the Pacific Ocean often runs into warmer air from near the equator. This creates strong winds that pull moisture from the air and drive it down to Earth. If the air becomes cold enough, this moisture will fall as ice or snow.

Canada, the United States, Russia, and China **lead the world in the number of blizzards.**

From 2000 to 2021, Walsh County in North Dakota was under a blizzard warning 84 times. That's almost four times a year—the most in the United States.

WHO DROVE AN OPEN-ROOF CAR TO COLORADO DURING WINTER?

WHOEVER IT WAS SURE LEARNED THEIR LESSON!

The one-day snowfall record in the United States was an incredible 76 in. (193 cm) that blanketed Colorado in 1921.

Moisture from the Great Lakes gives parts of New York State more snow than Alaska. This is called Lake Effect snow.

OH NO! GRAB THE SHOVELS! WE'RE GOING TO BE BUSY!

The colder the air, the drier it becomes. This is why the North Pole gets less snow than some parts of North America.

Syracuse, New York, is the snowiest city in the United States with an average of almost 128 in. (325 cm) every year.

To avoid blizzards, go to Fiji! The Pacific Island nation has never seen snow!

WHAT? I WAS TOLD HAWAII IS NOTHING BUT SUN AND BEACHES!

UM, AREN'T YOU A LITTLE UNDERDRESSED FOR THIS MOUNTAIN TRIP?

Unlike Fiji, the Hawaiian Islands do have blizzards. But they blow only at the tops of mountains.

Nasty Nor'easters

If you're looking for the perfect place to watch winter weather, hang out on the east coast of North America. In winter, polar air shoots across the plains of Canada and the United States all the way to the East Coast. There, it runs into warmer air sitting over the Atlantic Ocean and streaming up from the Gulf of Mexico. The result is a powerful, windy storm called a nor'easter that spins off the Atlantic coast like a hurricane. Instead of **torrential** rain, however, a winter nor'easter delivers heavy snow.

The Great Blizzard of 1888 was one of the worst in history. This nor'easter **slammed the Atlantic Coast from Virginia to Canada's Maritime provinces.**

Nor'easters are named for the coastal winds blowing from the northeast that drive the storms' rotation.

WOW! THAT'S ANOTHER CRAZY STORM FOR THE HISTORY BOOKS!

During the Great Blizzard, winds gusted up to 80 miles per hour (130 kph), and snow drifted into piles over 50 ft (15 m) tall.

Transportation troubles following the Great Blizzard inspired Boston and New York City to build subways that could keep running in bad weather.

Snowdrifts trapped 3,500 cars and trucks on a Massachusetts road during a 1978 nor'easter.

In 1996, a snowy nor'easter in Washington, D.C., **shut down the U.S. government for five days.**

Trick-or-treating was canceled after a nor'easter dumped feet of snow across New England from October 29–31, 2011.

Snow Monsters

Halloween snowstorms might seem a little scary, but the damage from blizzards can be truly frightening! Some monster blizzards knock out power lines, leaving schools, homes, and businesses without light or heat. Sometimes, roofs collapse under the weight of wet snow. Highways and airport runways can become covered with so much snow that they shut down. And people can get stuck in their homes or cars for days, with little food or water.

In 1972, a blizzard buried Iran in 26 feet (8 m) of **snow, killing 4,000 during the weeklong storm.**

During a 1978 blizzard, more than 5,000 Ohio National Guard soldiers rescued people trapped in their cars and homes.

In 1997, four blizzards brought heavy snow to Manitoba's Red River Valley. After the snow melted, the worst flooding in 100 years hit southern Manitoba, North Dakota, and Minnesota.

In 2015, blizzard winds pushed as much as 7 ft (2 m) of water onshore in Massachusetts, flooding homes and washing away seawalls.

The 2015 blizzard dumped 3 ft (90 cm) of snow in other parts of Massachusetts.

A 2022 blizzard brought more than 4 ft (1.2 m) of snow to Buffalo, NY, trapping many in their homes and cars. At least 40 people died in the storm.

Warmer but Snowier

Monster storms may be getting even more monstrous because of changes to Earth's climate. The planet is heating up as the **fuel** we burn to power our vehicles, homes, and businesses releases heat-trapping gases into the air. Unfortunately, having temperatures on the rise doesn't mean all snow will disappear. In some places, snowstorms may get even more intense. Warmer air holds more moisture. When this kind of air meets colder temperatures, more moisture can lead to heavier snow.

A warming planet may also make a windier planet. The warmer the air gets, the more violently it reacts when areas of high and low pressure come together. Blizzard winds may get even stronger.

Even the Arctic is heating up. In fact, it's warming up nearly four times faster than the rest of the world.

Sunlight bounces off white sea ice. When warmer air melts ice, the darker ocean is left uncovered. This takes in more heat, causing air and water temperatures to rise even higher.

Changes in the Arctic are sending more polar vortexes south.

Cold polar air mixing with moisture from the warming ocean can form monster blizzards like 2016's Snowzilla.

Snowzilla left 3 ft (90 cm) of snow in some Mid-Atlantic states, breaking snowfall records in Baltimore, D.C., Philadelphia, and New York City.

Getting ahead of the Storm

A warming planet and changing weather patterns make it harder to **predict** when a blizzard will form and how severe it will be. Computer models can show when wet weather is coming, but exact temperatures are hard to pin down. That's why it sometimes rains when meteorologists predict snow— or the other way around. But further study along with data from **satellites**, balloons, aircraft, and drones will help scientists make the best forecasts possible.

On March 11, 1888, the forecast in New York City was for cold winds but fair weather. **The next day, the city was buried under 4 ft (1.2 m) of snow!**

DON'T THEY KNOW THE DIFFERENCE BETWEEN AN INCH AND A FOOT?

I GUESS THEIR COMPUTERS NEED AN UPGRADE!

In 2000, computer models predicted an inch (2.5 cm) of snow for Washington, D.C. Instead, a blizzard dumped 18 in. (45 cm) of snow on the unprepared city.

Meteorologists aren't perfect, but they have a better record than Punxsutawney Phil. This groundhog predicts winter weather correctly less than half the time.

WHAT!?

YOU SAID THERE WOULD BE NO MORE SNOW!

DON'T TALK TO HIM. HE'S OBVIOUSLY CLUELESS!

Dogs are good forecasters! They may bark or alert in other ways before a blizzard hits because they can sense storms before humans do.

NASA's P-3 Orion plane has **sensors** under its wings **that measure clouds, snowflakes, temperature, and water vapor.**

DO WE NEED TO WORRY ABOUT THIS SNOWMAGEDDON?

I SHOULD THINK SO, WITH A NAME LIKE THAT!

Weather reporters often give the worst blizzards monstrous nicknames, such as Snozilla, Snowtastrophe, and Snowpocalypse.

Stay Home!

Knowing what's coming can help us prepare for a storm. Schools and businesses need time to decide if they should close down to keep people safe. Towns and cities need advance warning so snowplows can be ready and road crews can spread ice-melting materials on streets. Ordinary people need to pay attention to forecasts, too. When the National Weather Service declares a winter weather emergency, it's time to get off the streets and head home.

A Winter Storm Advisory means light snow is expected and everyone should be careful.

A Winter Storm Watch says there is a pretty good chance of major snow and ice, though it's not certain.

If you get a Winter Storm Warning, hunker down! A dangerous storm is headed your way.

A 2022 bomb cyclone set off blizzard warnings from Montana to New York. More than half of all Americans were under a severe weather warning.

Car accidents and slipping while walking on ice cause the most injuries during blizzards.

Blizzards often lead to massive multi-car accidents on highways. More than 100 vehicles piled up in March 2008 during a storm in the Czech Republic!

IT'S A SNOW DAY! WHY AREN'T YOU OUT PLAYING WITH YOUR FRIENDS?

Kids may not like it, but schools are turning snow days into at-home-learning days. No more breaks from school for them!

I WISH! THE GOOD OLD TIMES ARE OVER!

Sheltered and Safe

A little bit of warning means we have plenty of time to prepare to stay safe and warm in our homes during blizzards. What can you do to get ready if a storm is headed your way? Stock up on extra batteries, blankets, bottled water, and **nonperishable** food. If you do lose power, stay warm by wearing lots of layers. Keep your phone fully charged and have a portable charger so you can get safety updates and contact help if needed.

Keep an emergency kit handy. Fill it with first aid items, medications, snacks, water, important documents, and personal identification.

Be sure to stay **hydrated** if your heat goes out. This helps your body make heat and stay at a healthy temperature.

Learn where local **shelters** are in case you need to **evacuate** your home.

DO YOU KNOW WHERE THE SHELTER IS?

ABSOLUTELY! VERY CLEVER OF YOU TO ASK, SIR!

A Swedish man survived 60 days trapped in his snowbound car! He had only a sleeping bag and a few snacks with him.

After a severe 2022 blizzard, police officers in Erie County, NY, drove six hours to pick up baby food that families needed back home.

EXCUSE ME, I'M LOOKING FOR THE BARBER SHOP...

FOLLOW ME. I'M HEADING THERE MYSELF.

During that same blizzard, a Buffalo barber shop kept its doors open and became an emergency shelter for 50 people trapped by the storm.

Having a Meltdown

Activity

Icy roads and sidewalks are dangerous after a blizzard. Some people put down sand, salt, or chemicals to keep things from getting slippery. Which is the best way to deal with the ice and snow? Try this activity to find out.

Baking soda is a kind of salt.

What You Will Need

- 5 bowls
- 10 ice cubes
- A measuring spoon
- Salt
- Sugar
- Baking soda
- Sand

People sprinkle sand on ice to avoid slipping and sliding. The tiny pieces cling to ice and give better grip.

SUGAR

Baking Soda

Step One

Add two ice cubes to each bowl.

Step Two

Add two tablespoons of salt to one bowl, sugar to another, baking soda to a third, and sand to another. Leave one bowl with just ice.

Step Three

Observe your ice cubes after 15 minutes. Are any of the cubes melting faster than others?

Step Four

Check again after another 15 minutes. Make notes about which ice is melting fastest. Are any of the ice cubes melting more slowly than the ones without anything added?

Glossary

air pressure the force that is applied by the weight of the air

cyclones storms of winds that rotate or spin around a center of low air pressure

evacuate to leave a dangerous place

frigid extremely cold

fuel anything that can be burned to make energy

hydrated filled with enough water

meteorologists people who study the atmosphere, weather, and weather forecasting

nonperishable not likely to spoil or go bad

predict to make a guess ahead of time about something that will happen

rotation the turning of something around a central point

satellites space vehicles that travel around Earth and gather information

sensors machines that measure things, such as wind or heat

shelters places that offer cover, protection, and safety

squalls sudden, violent wind storms

tissues layers of cells, such as those that form our skin

torrential very heavy streaming or rushing

visibility a measure of the amount that can be seen

vortex something that moves in a circular or spiral pattern

Read More

Dalgleish, Sharon. *Blizzards (Severe Weather)*. Mendota Heights, MN: Apex, 2022.

Harris, Beatrice. *Blizzards (Rosen Verified: Natural Disasters)*. New York: Rosen Publishing, 2023.

McGregor, Harriet. *Blown Away by a Blizzard! (Uncharted: Stories of Survival)*. Minneapolis: Bearport Publishing, 2021.

Learn More Online

1. Go to **www.factsurfer.com** or scan the QR code below.

2. Enter **"X-treme Cold and Blizzards"** into the search box.

3. Click on the cover of this book to see a list of websites.

Index

About the Author

Marcia Abramson grew up and lives in Michigan. So, she knows blizzards.